MW00957430

twenty something

payton shelley

the triumphs and trials of falling in love with a boy, your

friends, and yourself

a compilation of poems displaying the most raw emotion that I

have been able to feel.

at 3am
i am inevitably finite,
destined to rest in hollowed dirt–

but in this crowded room,
full of people who dance:

i feel infinite.

weightless
i can feel the tarnished weight on my shoulders being lifted
each time your daunting eyes meet my fragile ones:

as if we are floating, and there isn't a bird in the sky.

light me up
you'd think it was
the fourth of july

with the way my stomach
get fireworks when i see you.

i just miss you
it's not fair that you get to start over.

-your daughter, remember her?

if only the birds could know
i think i love you,
and i think i shouldn't.

but oh how i want to run to the edge of the earth
and tell everyone–
anyone who *has* ever and *will* ever exist–
that i am in love with you.

how i wish even the trees could know,
for they could tell the birds for me.

sweet, sweet harmony
there is something about a rose's death
that heals the broken fire inside my body,

because the loss of something so beautiful
only creates space for more beautiful things.

youth and the loss of it
one year,
when my high school friends stop coming home from college,
i will say that i've grown up.

until then
we will spend summers together,
feeling eternally young.

long lasting memories
we will reminisce
when our children ask us about our lives.

the first time my heart felt broken
your laugh was like the smell of fresh rain
misting down onto an empty road:
>> beautiful and peaceful.

your words wrongly fill me with hope
then never ceased to exist
>> like i had hoped they would.

and your eyes, though piercing,
were as soft and light as cotton
>> yet with a hint of deceit.

you left as quickly as you came,
>> and soon it seemed as though every
brown-haired boy was you...

more than a midnight text
unlike those before you,
you don't care to listen
to my erratic what-ifs;

to wait until after
i have finished my rant
to tell me i was in the wrong;

to sit with me and talk
about everything and nothing
for hours and hours;

to lay, your hand in mine,
breathing the same occupied air,
our hearts beating in rhythm.

unlike those before you,
my body is not a prerequisite
for all of these beautiful things.

i think i must have made you up.

mom? i heard the birds chirping again this morning.
i've spent all these years dreading to get up

but you,
you make waking up
feel like a reward.

admitting to myself that i am in love with you
i claimed that my lust
was purely a fraction
of lost opportunities

until your eyes met hers
the way they used to
look at me.

i became sick
as though the liquor
had shot through my stomach

and as she leaned in to whisper into your ear,
i could see nothing
but for the first time in years,
i could feel everything.

i am in love with you

you're everywhere i look.
when i've decided
that your absence
no longer controls
my ability to smile;

when i start to forget
the little things about you
that i dwelled on
for weeks after it ended;

and just when your face
stops creeping into every thought,
your eyes into every glance,
and your body into every movement,

someone says your name.

and it all floods back.

before i learned that a broken heart can be put back together
you looked into my eyes
and made a broken promise
and i let you get away
with ruining my perception of love.

begging someone to love me
broken–to start with,
yet so eager to be fixed.

her head on a pedestal
and her heart in her hands.

from the kid of a broken home, who hates the idea of marriage
i'm starting to get why marriage is appealing.

the biggest,
most profound proclamation
of unconditional love.

it is the ultimate
"i love you."

and i think i understand why people get married.

taking a risk, and being okay with a failure
and if this doesn't work out
i will never regret falling in love with you
because the world looks different now,
and i now know that i am capable of feeling this.

**alcoholic tendencies that i picked up from having my heart
broken, for real this time.**
i would rather scarf down
fiery liquids that burn my throat
and make me sick to my stomach,

than have to think about you
and the way i felt
when you had your hands all over her.

and when you still talk to her sometimes,
i try my hardest
to not reach for the bottle

because feeling nothing
is a thousand times more tolerable
than feeling whatever it is i do when you hurt me.

let yourself go, but not too much
in the midst of falling in love,
i seemed to distance myself from things i used to adore.

i wonder, sometimes,
if part of me is gone forever.

i lost part of myself,
and i'm working on getting her back.

when you're gone
when i can't sleep at night
      i find myself wondering
if your hand misses mine
      the way mine misses yours.

before i fell in love
some days,
i feel like my indifference to love is not because i think i'm
incapable of loving,
but that i am incapable of being loved.

maybe i act like i hate it
because i know that it hates me.

breathing in the water that drowns me
what is life–
if not a task...
a long, never-ending
ruthless task.

some days i feel as though i'm a fish in a tainted water–
a tainted water full of fish who have grown accustomed to their
surroundings,
and i have fallen behind.

i never learned what to do in tainted water.

i love you i love you i love you
i often ponder our love–
what drew you to me?
what drew me to you?

i think somehow the stars just knew.
and then they led me to you.

there was a universal pull that brought us together,
i have no doubt about it.
how else would it have been so strong–
right from the start?

an empty sea, we lay in the middle
"there are plenty of fish in the sea."

if there are plenty,
why do we stay here?
looking out to the water:
i only see you.

knock knock. it's me again.
every time i thought i was done,
each time i decided i was sweeping my brain of your voice—
you smile at me across the room
and i forget all the terrible things you made me feel.

sometimes the good is so good
that the bad is irrevocably irrelevant.

"total abandonment. i give myself."
i cannot fathom a love without you.

for i would sooner be a desolate soul,
than love another the way i love you.

new york, new york.
i contemplate my decision to discard my incredible,
once-in-a-lifetime opportunity that i was granted last year.
often, i wonder what my life would have been like if i had
followed my dreams.
i think about my younger self, who would be absolutely appalled
that i gave up such an enormously impossible opportunity that
pointed me in the exact direction of my dreams, setting me up
for perfect–and almost guaranteed–success.

but the me that would have gone to new york...
she would have hated it.
and she would have hated herself every day,
lonely as ever.

part of me wishes i had tried.
and that same part of me remembers the 8 year old girl that i let
down by not going.

but i didn't go.
and,
i have to be okay with that.

New York,
New York

there's a stranger in my mirror
i don't remember who i am
did *i* do that to me?
is this *my* doing?

i can't remember the last time i did something for myself.

regrets

recently, my regrets follow me like a shadow,
like a fever i can't break–
like a child who doesn't know any better.

my regrets often whisper in my ear
right when i decide i'm finally happy–
just when i think i might be able to start painting again.

my regrets chase me through an old alleyway
and they corner me in the dim light.

my regrets ask me one thing:
what would 10-year-old you
say about this pathetic life you're living?

i think deep down, 10-year-old me might've loved this...
but she would've been just like me–
her regrets would have followed her like a shadow.

when is it ok to start listening to my regrets?

on my knees
sometimes you have to beg someone to love you
and sometimes they think they're already doing it.

i scorch my back with the fire in your words.
my body burns from the inside out with your nonchalant
neglect.
i ask relentlessly for a change–
and the flame on my back grows in size.

sometimes, the burn reminds me of the bad days
and of my favorite lighter i kept on my bedside table.
and maybe that's why
i've never stopped you from wounding me

i keep begging you to love me.
how do i know when to give up?

pretty
you only ever call me pretty
when i'm naked and lying under you.

only then am i pretty.

everything i thought i knew
recently i've felt like i'm sitting
in the middle of a cardboard room—
and the cardboard walls around me
have all started to fall in unison—
no turns or breaks
but all at once.

as they fall they catch fire,
and i stay put—
as if i am glued to floor,
infinitely stationary.

i don't know how to leave
because this cardboard room is all i have ever known.

homesick

i've reached the point in life
where nowhere feels like home.

home is not with my mom
and it's not with my dad.

home is not in my house
with my boyfriend and my cats.

home is not my first apartment
with my two best friends.

my home is an idea—
a nostalgic idea i once had
and i've forgotten how to remember it.

god. i want to go home.

texts i never sent
i'm sorry.

-your old best friend.

when i lost myself to trying
lately i have lost any ability
to recognize myself in a crowd.

any memory i have of myself is gone—
shredded to pieces
like it had never existed in the first place.

it's almost as if the person who knows me best
has never been myself.

they'll ask "what's your favorite color"
...why will i not know the answer?

"i'm so proud of you"
sometimes that's all i wanted to hear—
that someone saw me trying
and was proud of that.

it seems,
more and more each day,
like you know
just exactly what to say.

you are always so angry
sometimes i'm reminded of my weekends as a child–
we'll be sitting on the couch and all of a sudden you are mad,
and i'm the only culprit around.
and that is how my weekends went.

sometimes i feel like i never grew up:
i never moved on,
like i'm still getting yelled at–
and i don't understand what i did wrong.

i'm just a kid.
and i don't understand what i did to make you so angry.

you're supposed to understand more as you get older,
but i still don't understand.

barbie by greta gerwig
when i was 5 i thought i could do anything
and now that i'm 20 i feel like i can't do anything at all.

little me thought she could be
a doctor
a teacher
a singer
an actress
a lawyer.

now little me is just me—
and i have no idea what i was made for.

i saw an old friend today
her smile brought me back to the old days
when we would laugh on the school bus
and in the backyard.

she embraced me without hesitation,
never once thinking about the time that has passed,
and the possible awkwardness to come from the loss—
but there was none.

it was like no time had passed,
we were still sitting in class
laughing when we shouldn't be,
talking quietly so as not to get caught.

we say "let's catch up"
when we both know we never will.
but the gesture seems nice from both ends,
letting the other know we still care.

old friend,
sometimes you cross my mind.

texts i never sent pt 2
i never meant to hurt you,
but it seems that's all i knew how to do then.

decorations
i poke the needle to my skin
over and over
creating dazzling, yet crooked lines
with the tiny little dots of ink.

i patch up empty spots
along each limb,
coating them in beautiful, new,
original images.

it is beautiful to have a blank canvas
and to paint it however you would like...

what is this body for,
if not to decorate?

harry potter and the anxiety-ridden girl
i used to be ashamed of my wishful longing–
the wishes i made on shooting stars,
the nights i prayed to anyone who would listen,
that i could escape to a beautiful world that didn't exist.

on the nights that were especially hard,
i would dream of being free.
of being in a magical land where
anything is possible.

i never seemed to grow out of it.
i never stopped escaping to imaginary worlds
to forget about the hard days i had...

sometimes i can still hear the wistful birds,
and the sounds of magic when i close my eyes at night.

sometimes i think they still call to me the way they did when i
was young.

acknowledgements

I struggled for a long time to find a way to express the things I was feeling. One year of college, I took a creative writing class and I was assigned to write a few poems. I fell in love. I have always loved writing and it has always been such a big part of my life but I never realized I could work through my feelings through my own writing. So I did just that.

Writing makes it a lot easier to deal with things and I love sharing my writing with other people. I'm so excited to be able to put this book in the world. It has been a dream of mine to hold a book in my hands that I wrote–*me*. I can now finally say that I can do that. It may be small but it holds a lot of years in it. I hope you–whoever you are–will take in the poems I've written and feel the way we are supposed to feel. The way I have always been so afraid of.

I found myself afraid of a lot as a kid and as I've gotten older the fears don't ever really go away, but they subside a little bit. They turn from an overwhelming, overpowering, breathtaking-in-the-bad way fear, to a dull ache in the back of my mind that only shows up sometimes.

I thought I would never make it out of sixteen. I thought I would drive myself crazy and feel too much and see too much and never want to keep going. But I love feeling everything again. I love to walk around without the blanket covering my heart and making everything numb. I love smiling and laughing. I love crying and being angry. I love feeling everything we are supposed to feel.

I think my poems capture it all–the hurt, the jealousy, falling in love for the first time, and then the second, being angry, being sad, feeling lonely, being happy, and being so over-the-moon you don't know what to do with yourself. I hope you enjoyed the book as much as I enjoyed writing it. It lives in a part of my heart and I think it will remain there even after the sun swallows the Earth.

Made in the USA
Las Vegas, NV
20 December 2024

14941873R10035